Arthur Landsman

Strategy Implementation. Health Care Sector SickKids

Stragetic Planning SickKids Hospital

GRIN Publishing

Bibliographic information published by the German National Library:

The German National Library lists this publication in the National Bibliography; detailed bibliographic data are available on the Internet at http://dnb.dnb.de .

Imprint:

Copyright © 2013 GRIN Verlag GmbH
Print and binding: Books on Demand GmbH, Norderstedt Germany
ISBN: 978-3-656-87106-4

This book at GRIN:

http://www.grin.com/en/e-book/286592/strategy-implementation-health-care-sector-sickkids

Strategy Implementation

Arthur Landsman
CASP 200
Strategic Planning

July 29th, 2013

Introduction

After the strategies have been developed and formulated for the organization, the following stage of the strategic planning process is the implementation of the strategic plan. This must take into account the effective and smooth implementation of the organization's strategic plan in order to fulfill the public value aimed to be created during the formulation process. The four mechanisms to implement strategies include: programs, projects, action plans, and budgets. As stated by Bryson, "developing effective programs, projects, action plans, budgets and implementation processes will bring life to the strategies and create more tangible and intangible value for the organization and its stakeholders."[1] The following will review how the current strategic plan for SickKids, "Avenues to Excellence: 2010-2015," has been implemented. The paper will show how SickKids has utilized various programs, projects, action plans, and budgets to implement the six strategies outlined in its current strategic plan.

Strategies

As outlined in the SickKids "Avenues to Excellence" strategic plan for 2010-2015, the six strategies include:[2]

Strategic Direction #1	Lead in World-Class Quality and Service Excellence
Strategic Direction #2	Enable Our People
Strategic Direction #3	Innovate
Strategic Direction #4	Maintain Financial Health
Strategic Direction #5	Build Sustainable Infrastructure
Strategic Direction #6	Enhance Child Health Systems

These can then be further dived as grand strategies, functional strategies, and sub-unit strategies. The first grand strategies for SickKids are to Lead in World-Class Quality and Service Excellence and Enhance Child Health Systems. The functional strategies consist of Enable Our People and Building Sustainable Infrastructure. Lastly, the Sub-unit strategies consist of Maintain Financial Health and Innovation. This is the order that the paper will continue to examine the various strategies.

Programs, Projects, Action Plans & Budgets

It becomes necessary to briefly outline what a program, project, action plan, and budget is before describing the ones used by SickKids. The difference between a program and a project is the duration of the both, whereas programs tend to be ongoing activities that can extend an indefinite period of time, projects, on the other hand, are temporary in nature and are designed to deliver a specific result for the company.[3] Projects have a "specific beginning date and end-date, specific objective and specific resources assigned to perform the work."[4] Programs are also "groups of related, ongoing activities that are designed and managed to meet specific, defined needs."[5] Action plans can be seen as "a series of actions, tasks or steps designed to achieve an objective or goal."[6] Budgets comprise of detailed reports of income and expenditures over a period of one year.[7]

Lead in World Class Quality and Service Excellence

In order to implement SickKids' first strategic priority, the hospital intends to establish a program that will create guiding principles for service excellence in both clinical areas of the organization as well as non-clinical areas.[8] The intended purpose is to ingrain these principles into the culture of the organization in order to create a culture of service excellence.[9]

SickKids also has a project to optimize patient safety, as noted in the *Blueprint for Patient Safety*, it will implement ten building blocks for safe patient care. The program will also collaborate with the University of Toronto's Centre for Patient Safety in research areas involving patient safety and in the development of "wide-ranging education and training programs."[10] SickKids also plans to design a program that will allow access to health care for children from various backgrounds, underprivileged communities, and socio-economic levels.[11] It will involve professionals from the field that will work together to develop strategies to ensure that the most vulnerable in society have access to appropriate care, and facilities such as "emergency, surgical, inpatient and ambulatory care."[12]

The next program is designed around performance management. The *Enterprise Performance Management* program is "a disciplined process for measuring the performance of all clinical care, research, education, operational programs and services against stated objectives and targets."[13] It will use scorecards and dashboards in its reporting to assess the abovementioned and to support its enterprise performance management system.[14]

Enhance Child Health Systems

In order to enhance child health systems as outlined in the SickKids strategic plan, SickKids hospital intends to build strategic partnerships and to find means to collaborate internally in its own organization. SickKids has employed a program called the "Centre Model," which it will utilize to "enhance collaboration and integration within the organization."[15] It will do so by promoting collaboration between health professionals, as well as advancing future policy.

SickKids International is a program that establishes collaboration between international partners. It has three activities globally that fall under: Global Child Health Program, Business Development and the International Patient Office.[16] The *Global Child Health Program (GCHP)* works in vulnerable communities in low and middle income countries in order to strengthen local health systems.[17] It works in countries such as Ghana, Ethiopia, and other sub-Saharan African countries. One of the many programs and projects that fall under the GCHP is the *CIDA-SickKids Global Child Health Program.* It is a partnership between the Canadian International Development Agency (CIDA), the SickKids Foundation, and SickKids hospital. Its goal is to "strengthen the capacity of paediatric health-care systems and promote child health leadership in sub-Saharan Africa."[18] It currently has two ongoing programs taking place in sub-Saharan Africa. *The Ghana-SickKids Paediatric Nursing Training Programme* is an attempt to train 1,000 to 1,500 Paediatric Nurses in the West African country of Ghana.[19] *The Ethiopia-SickKids Paediatric Nurse Practitioner Training Programme* is a similar program designed to develop Nurse Practitioners in the country of Ethiopia.[20] The *Public Engagement in Canada* project is a project designed to spread awareness about global child health issues to young Canadians.[21] In addition, the *Programme for Global Paediatric Research* (PGPR) also falls under the GCHP set of programs and projects. It aims to bring together paediatric researchers from around the world in order to help alleviate child health issues in developing countries around the world.[22] It works with networks such as the Global Sickle Cell Disease network and the Global Prevention of Kernicterus Network.[23] *The Caribbean-SickKids Paediatric Cancer and Blood*

Disorders Strategy is a project that will attempt to build a network of specialists in the Caribbean region to help improve the quality of life for children with cancer and blood disorders.[24] The *SickKids No Boundaries* is a program that focuses on paediatric surgical care for children in developing countries by collaborating between surgical specialists around the world.[25]

The second activity of SickKids International is the Business Development division. It utilizes its diverse network of skilled medical professionals to provide advisory services to governments across the world, organizations, and institutions. Its various projects and programs include advisory services in the country of Qatar, where it is engaged in a 5-year partnership project with the Hamad Medical Corporation in order provide advisory services for the development of a new children's hospital in the city.[26] It further has a multi-year project in India with the Madanmohan Ruia Raptakos Children's Hospital (MRRCH) to provide advisory services in phases, which it is currently in stage 2 of the project.[27] These advisory services include; "clinical and functional plans, medical equipment and information technology."[28] Lastly, it has a project established in Ireland to provide advisory services to the development of the national tertiary centre for an 8-year period.[29] The *International Learner Program* (ILP) is an educational service designed to allow international health-care professionals to gain experience at the SickKids hospital, through such areas as practice, education, research, and administration, and then apply their acquired skills back in their home countries.[30] Furthermore, the International Health Assignment Workshop (IHAW) provides health-care professionals with training in international health issues.[31]

The third activity consists of the International Patient Office and the subsequent *International Patient Program* which works with international patients who come to the hospital in Toronto to receive specialized treatment. It provides a series of services to the children before their procedure, these include; medical review, financial assessment, family support and case management."[32]

Enable Our People

The *New Immigrant Support Network (NISN)* is a program that consists of two subsequent projects: Cultural Competence Education and Translation of Patient Resources and Materials.[33] Cultural Competence Education is a workshop that aims to teach cultural differences between SickKids staff members. The Translation of Patient Resources and Materials is a partnership with AboutKidsHealth, the project aims to translate "300 key health-related patient education resources and other materials into French, simplified and traditional Chinese, Arabic, Spanish, Tamil, Urdu, Portuguese and Punjabi.[34] It also includes audio translation in the above stated languages.[35]

In order to facilitate skill growth and leadership development SickKids has an action plan to implement "innovative" programs that will help staff learn to become capable leaders and managers. It aims to "implement succession planning in a rigorous, planned fashion to ensure an ongoing supply of talented leaders ready to address current and future needs."[36] In addition, SickKids plans to implement a set of balanced programs that support the health and well-being of its staff, and to keep the workplace safe for its employees through the reduction of employee illness and workplace accidents.[37] It will also recognize and reward its leaders through a recognition program that will reward staff members for their contributions to the hospital in its many faculties. It will develop and implement performance assessment tools that will help recognize those that contribute to the organization.[38]

Build Sustainable Infrastructure

In order to renew its facilities to meet future demands, SickKids has engaged in the project of building the *SickKids Research and Learning Tower*. The Research Tower is expected to be completed in 2013, after construction for the tower started in May 2010.[39] It will comprise of a new 750,000 square foot facility built in Toronto's Discovery District.[40] The project is expected to cost an estimated $400 million, $200 million dollars of which are part of a fundraising campaign conducted by the SickKids Foundation.[41] The hospital itself has reserved $93.0 million in capital for the onset of the project.[42] The tower will also connect the SickKids science and discovery centre to its clinical operations.[43] It will provide SickKids researchers a place to exchange ideas and improve health care for children.

In order to develop comprehensive and coordinated eHealth strategy, SickKids will engage in a project in conjunction with the Ministry of Health and Long-Term Care and various agencies to overhaul the eCHN[2] electronic health record system for the province.[44] This will allow for patient information to be more easily distributed to various doctors and medical facilities.[45] To further upgrade and invest in new technologies it will also "invest in medical equipment, information systems and core technologies that will enhance and integrate with existing technologies in order to achieve a fully integrated patient care information system."[46]

SickKids will also implement environmentally friendly programs, such as the "procurement and delivery of environmentally-safe products and services, the promotion of energy and resource utilization efficiency, the reduction of waste and pollution, improvements to hazardous waste disposal and the greening of the SickKids workplace, patient care, and research environments."[47] General physical infrastructure improvements will also be made to the hospital under the Master Plan program, which will be implemented in phases.[48]

Budgets

As Bryson states, budgets are one of the most important tools for strategic implementation. The allocation of resources in an organization is "perhaps the most telling way of understanding that organization's strategic priorities."[49] As stated in the SickKids strategic plan, it recognizes the importance of budgeting when implementing strategy. It sees that there can be a financial barrier to budgeting, as 60% of organizations do not link budgets to strategy.[50] There is also a resources barrier, when resources are spread too thin over many strategic projects.[51]

Maintain Financial Health

SickKids' priority is to balance its financial plan from 2010-2012 through increasing revenues, investing strategically, and collaborating with the SickKids Foundation. In order to generate increased revenues SickKids will implement revenue generation activities from funds that are received from "the Ministry of Health and Long-Term Care, Toronto Central LHIN and other funders... ."[52] Currently at "$447.6 million, funding from the Ministry of Health and Long-Term Care (MOHLTC) and the Toronto Central Local Health Integration Network (TC LHIN) is SickKids' most significant source of income, representing 61.8% of total revenues.[53] SickKids will also invest its funds strategically in order to generate revenues for the hospital; it will do so through an integrated risk management framework.[54] As can be seen in the hospital's balance sheet, investment income from 2011 to 2012 went up 285.5% after implementing invest strategies from its strategic plan.[55] (See appendix A)

SickKids will align its fundraising strategies and programs with the SickKids Foundation. The Foundation, which is the fund-raising arm for the SickKids hospital, provides a large portion of the hospital's budgets for its programs, projects and initiatives. It currently has more than 265,000 donors and in 2011-2012 more than 1,880 grant-funded research projects taking place.[56] As of March 31, 2012, the SickKids Foundation invested $61.3 million into the SickKids hospital in child health research, learning and care.[57] It consists mostly of private donations from individuals, families, companies, and other foundations and does not include funding that SickKids receives from the government or grants.[58]

Innovate

In order to maintain and develop its culture of innovation, SickKids has various action plans designed to implement its strategy of innovation. It has a plan to allow "open access to information" for staff to freely exchange ideas.[59] Moreover, there is a program that allows for the free exchange of innovative new ideas from both internal and external sources. These ideas will be screened by senior staff managers and if accepted will be fully funded in order to be incorporated into the SickKids organization.[60] SickKids is also exploring the idea of instituting a program that would commercialize some of its research priorities and developments. This research includes; "many avenues including technology spin-offs, patents and licensing agreements."[61]

Conclusion

Strategy implementation is an important component of the strategic planning process. As Bryson states, "without effective implementation, important issues will not be adequately addressed and lasting tangible public value will not be created."[62] SickKids has instituted various programs, projects, action plans, and budgets to implement the six strategic directives outlined in its strategic plan. It has chosen to implement plans both internally and externally to fulfill its initiatives. It has instituted many global programs and projects in order to collaborate with health professionals and centres around the world. It has also instituted many internal programs to enhance its own services, better care for its patients, support its staff members, and build new infrastructures and technologies. The next step of the strategic planning process is to examine the strategic management system that SickKids has instituted to manage the implementation of these strategies.

Endnotes

[1] John M. Bryson, "Implementing Strategies and Plans Successfully," Strategic Planning: For Public and Nonprofit Organization, 2011, p. 286
[2] SickKids, "Avenues to Excellence 2010-2015," <http://www.sickkids.ca/pdfs/About-SickKids/Avenues-to-Excellence/24174-SickKids-Strategic-Plan.pdf> p.26
[3] Class Notes
[4] Ibid.
[5] Class Notes.
[6] Ibid.
[7] Ibid.
[8] SickKids, "Avenues to Excellence 2010-2015," <http://www.sickkids.ca/pdfs/About-SickKids/Avenues-to-Excellence/24174-SickKids-Strategic-Plan.pdf> p.22
[9] Ibid.
[10] Ibid.
[11] SickKids, "Avenues to Excellence 2010-2015," <http://www.sickkids.ca/pdfs/About-SickKids/Avenues-to-Excellence/24174-SickKids-Strategic-Plan.pdf> p.22
[12] Ibid.
[13] Ibid.
[14] Ibid.
[15] SickKids, "Avenues to Excellence 2010-2015," <http://www.sickkids.ca/pdfs/About-SickKids/Avenues-to-Excellence/24174-SickKids-Strategic-Plan.pdf> p.25
[16] SickKids, "SickKids International," The Hospital for Sick Children, 1999-2012, web. 15 June 2012, <http://www.sickkids.ca/sickkidsinternational>.
[17] SickKids, "SickKids International," The Hospital for Sick Children, 1999-2012, web. 15 June 2012, <http://www.sickkids.ca/sickkidsinternational/aboutSKI/AreasofFocus/Areas-of-Focus.html>.
[18] SickKids International, "Global Child Health Program," The Hospital for Sick Children, 1999 2012, web. 10 July 2012, < http://www.sickkids.ca/sickkidsinternational/38571-SickKids%20GCHP%20factsheet%20Nov2011.pdf> p.2
[19] Ibid.
[20] Ibid.
[21] Ibid.
[22] SickKids International, "Programme for Global Paediatric Research," The Hospital for Sick Children, 1999-2012, web. 10 July 2012, <http://www.sickkids.ca/sickkidsinternational/GCHP/PGPR/PGPR.html>
[23] Ibid.
[24] SickKids International, "Global Child Health Program," The Hospital for Sick Children, 1999 2012, web. 10 July 2012, < http://www.sickkids.ca/sickkidsinternational/38571-SickKids%20GCHP%20factsheet%20Nov2011.pdf> p.2
[25] SickKids International. "SickKids No Boundaries." The Hospital for Sick Children, 1999-2012. Web. 10 July 2012. < http://www.sickkids.ca/sickkidsinternational/GCHP/SickKids-No-Boundaries/SickKids-No-Boundaries.html>
[26] SickKids International, "Business Development: Qatar," The Hospital for Sick Children, 1999 2012, web. 10 July 2012 <http://www.sickkids.ca/sickkidsinternational/businessdevelopment/Qatar/Qatar.html>
[27] SickKids International, "Business Development," The Hospital for Sick Children, 1999-2012,

web. 10 July 2012 < http://www.sickkids.ca/sickkidsinternational/38572-SickKids%20BD%20factsheet%20Nov2011.pdf>

[28] SickKids International, "Business Development: India," The Hospital for Sick Children, 1999 2012. Web. 10 July 2012. <http://www.sickkids.ca/sickkidsinternational/businessdevelopment/India/India.html>.

[29] SickKids International, "Business Development," The Hospital for Sick Children, 1999-2012, web. 10 July 2012 < http://www.sickkids.ca/sickkidsinternational/38572-SickKids%20BD%20factsheet%20Nov2011.pdf>

[30] SickKids International, "International Learner Program," The Hospital for Sick Children, 1999 2012, web. 10 July 2012 < http://www.sickkids.ca/sickkidsinternational/learning-opportunities/ILP/International-Learner-Program.html>.

[31] SickKids International, "Business Development," The Hospital for Sick Children, 1999-2012, web. 10 July 2012 < http://www.sickkids.ca/sickkidsinternational/38572-SickKids%20BD%20factsheet%20Nov2011.pdf>

[32] SickKids International, "International Patient Office," The Hospital for Sick Children, 19992012, web. 10 July 2012 < http://www.sickkids.ca/sickkidsinternational/38573-SickKids%20IPO%20factsheet%20Nov2011.pdf>.

[33] SickKids, "About NISN," 1999-2012, The Hospital for Sick Children, web. 15 June 2012 <http://www.sickkids.ca/culturalcompetence/About-NISN/about-nisn.html>.

[34] Ibid.

[35] Ibid.

[36] SickKids, "Avenues to Excellence 2010-2015," <http://www.sickkids.ca/pdfs/About-SickKids/Avenues-to-Excellence/24174-SickKids-Strategic-Plan.pdf> p.18

[37] Ibid.

[38] SickKids, "Avenues to Excellence 2010-2015," <http://www.sickkids.ca/pdfs/About-SickKids/Avenues-to-Excellence/24174-SickKids-Strategic-Plan.pdf> p.19.

[39] About SickKids, "SickKids Research & Learning Tower springs up from the ground," 2012, The Hospital for Sick Children, Web. 10 July 2012, <http://www.sickkids.ca/AboutSickKids/Newsroom/Past-News/2011/Tower-to-grade-web-story.html>.

[40] Build SickKids, "SickKids Centre for Research and Learning Tower: Quick Facts," 2012, The Hospital for Sick Children, Web 5 July 2012, < http://www.buildsickkids.com/quickfacts.asp>.

[41] SickKids Foundation, "SickKids Fact Book 2011-2012," The SickKids Foundation, web 12 July 2012, <http://www.sickkidsfoundation.com/togive/downloads/SKF_Fact_Book_1112.pdf> p. 14-15.

[42] SickKids, "Financial Position and Management for the year ended March 31, 2012," The Hospital for Sick Children, 1999-2012, web 15 July 2012 < http://www.sickkids.ca/pdfs/About-SickKids/yearinreview20112012/44564-Financial%20Overview%20-%202011-2012.pdf> p.2

[43] About SickKids, "SickKids Research & Learning Tower springs up from the ground," 2012, The Hospital for Sick Children, Web. 10 July 2012, <http://www.sickkids.ca/AboutSickKids/Newsroom/Past-News/2011/Tower-to-grade-web-story.html>.

[44] SickKids, "Avenues to Excellence 2010-2015," <http://www.sickkids.ca/pdfs/About-SickKids/Avenues-to-Excellence/24174-SickKids-Strategic-Plan.pdf> p.19

[45] SickKids, "Avenues to Excellence 2010-2015," <http://www.sickkids.ca/pdfs/About-SickKids/Avenues-to-Excellence/24174-SickKids-Strategic-Plan.pdf> p.7

[46] SickKids, "Avenues to Excellence 2010-2015," <http://www.sickkids.ca/pdfs/About-SickKids/Avenues-to-Excellence/24174-SickKids-Strategic-Plan.pdf> p.19

[47] SickKids, "Avenues to Excellence 2010-2015," <http://www.sickkids.ca/pdfs/About-SickKids/Avenues-to-Excellence/24174-SickKids-Strategic-Plan.pdf> p.20

[48] SickKids, "Avenues to Excellence 2010-2015," <http://www.sickkids.ca/pdfs/About-SickKids/Avenues-to-Excellence/24174-SickKids-Strategic-Plan.pdf> p.19

[49] Janet Lunn, "PAPD 504: Module 6 Strategy Implementation," Humber College, Toronto, Ontario, 5 Sept 2010, p. 1

[50] SickKids, "Avenues to Excellence 2010-2015," <http://www.sickkids.ca/pdfs/About-SickKids/Avenues-to-Excellence/24174-SickKids-Strategic-Plan.pdf> p.13

[51] Ibid.

[52] SickKids, "Avenues to Excellence 2010-2015," <http://www.sickkids.ca/pdfs/About-SickKids/Avenues-to-Excellence/24174-SickKids-Strategic-Plan.pdf> p.21

[53] SickKids, "Financial Position and Management for the year ended March 31, 2012," The Hospital for Sick Children, 1999-2012, web 15 July 2012 < http://www.sickkids.ca/pdfs/About-SickKids/yearinreview20112012/44564-Financial%20Overview%20-%202011-2012.pdf> p 1.

[54] SickKids, "Avenues to Excellence 2010-2015," <http://www.sickkids.ca/pdfs/About-SickKids/Avenues-to-Excellence/24174-SickKids-Strategic-Plan.pdf> p.21

[55] SickKids, "Financial Position and Management for the year ended March 31, 2012," The Hospital for Sick Children, 1999-2012, web 15 July 2012 < http://www.sickkids.ca/pdfs/About-SickKids/yearinreview20112012/44564-Financial%20Overview%20-%202011-2012.pdf> p 1.

[56] SickKids Foundation, "SickKids Fact Book 2011-2012," The SickKids Foundation, web 12 July 2012, <http://www.sickkidsfoundation.com/togive/downloads/SKF_Fact_Book_1112.pdf> p. 11

[57] SickKids Foundation, "About Us," The SickKids Foundation, web 10 July 2012, <http://www.sickkidsfoundation.com/aboutus/>

[58] Ibid.

[59] SickKids, "Avenues to Excellence 2010-2015," <http://www.sickkids.ca/pdfs/About-SickKids/Avenues-to-Excellence/24174-SickKids-Strategic-Plan.pdf> p.23

[60] Ibid.

[61] Ibid.

[56] John M. Bryson, "Implementing Strategies and Plans Successfully," Strategic Planning: For Public and Nonprofit Organization, 2011, p. 316.

Works Cited

About SickKids. "SickKids Research & Learning Tower springs up from the ground," 2012, The Hospital for Sick Children, Web. 10 July 2012. <http://www.sickkids.ca/AboutSickKids/Newsroom/Past-News/2011/Tower-to-grade-web-story.html>.

"Avenues to Excellence 2010-2015." *The Hospital for Sick Children Strategic Plan*. Jan. 2010. Web 5 July 2012. <http://www.sickkids.ca/pdfs/About-SickKids/Avenues-to-Excellence/24174-SickKids-Strategic-Plan.pdf>.

Bryson, John M. "Implementing Strategies and Plans Successfully." Strategic Planning: For Public and Nonprofit Organization. 4th ed. San Francisco: Jossey-Bass, 2011. 286-316.

Build SickKids. "SickKids Centre for Research and Learning Tower," 2012, The Hospital for Sick Children, Web 5 July 2012. < http://www.buildsickkids.com>.

SickKids. "About NISN," 1999-2012, The Hospital for Sick Children, Web. 15 June 2012 <http://www.sickkids.ca/culturalcompetence/About-NISN/about-nisn.html>.

SickKids. "Financial Position and Management for the year ended March 31, 2012," The Hospital for Sick Children, 1999-2012. Web 15 July 2012 < http://www.sickkids.ca/pdfs/About-SickKids/yearinreview20112012/44564-Financial%20Overview%20-%202011-2012.pdf>.

SickKids. "Financial Statements: March 31st, 2012," The Hospital for Sick Children, 1999-2012. Web. 01 July 2012. < http://www.sickkids.ca/pdfs/About-SickKids/yearinreview20112012/44464-HSC%20Financial%20Statements%20-%20March%2031%202012%20pdf2.pdf>.

SickKids. "The Centre for Genetic Medicine," The Hospital for Sick Children, Web. 12 July 2012 < http://www.sickkids.ca/Centres/Centre-Genetic-Medicine/index.html>.

SickKids. "SickKids International," *SickKids,* The Hospital for Sick Children, 1999-2012. Web. 15 June 2012. <http://www.sickkids.ca/sickkidsinternational>.

SickKids Foundation. "Annual Report: 2011-2012." The SickKids Foundation. Web 18 July 2012.

<http://www.sickkidsfoundation.com/togive/downloads/SKF_Annual_Report_1112.pdf>.

SickKids Foundation. "About Us." The SickKids Foundation. Web 10 July 2012 <http://www.sickkidsfoundation.com/aboutus/>.

SickKids Foundation. "SickKids Fact Book 2011-2012." The SickKids Foundation. Web 12 July 2012.
<http://www.sickkidsfoundation.com/togive/downloads/SKF_Fact_Book_1112.pdf>.

SickKids International. "Business Development," The Hospital for Sick Children, 1999-2012. Web. 10 July 2012. < http://www.sickkids.ca/sickkidsinternational/38572-SickKids%20BD%20factsheet%20Nov2011.pdf>.

SickKids International. "Business Development: India," The Hospital for Sick Children, 1999 2012. Web. 10 July 2012. < http://www.sickkids.ca/sickkidsinternational/businessdevelopment/India/India.html >.

SickKids International. "Business Development: Qatar," The Hospital for Sick Children, 1999 2012. Web. 10 July 2012. <http://www.sickkids.ca/sickkidsinternational/businessdevelopment/Qatar/Qatar.ht ml>

SickKids International. "Global Child Health Program," The Hospital for Sick Children, 1999 2012. Web. 10 July 2012. < http://www.sickkids.ca/sickkidsinternational/38571-SickKids%20GCHP%20factsheet%20Nov2011.pdf>.

SickKids International. "International Health Assignment Workshop," The Hospital for Sick Children, 1999-2012. Web. 10 July 2012. <http://www.sickkids.ca/sickkidsinternational/learning-opportunities/IHAW/IHAW.html>.

SickKids International. "International Learner Program," The Hospital for Sick Children, 1999 2012. Web. 10 July 2012. < http://www.sickkids.ca/sickkidsinternational/learning-opportunities/ILP/International-Learner-Program.html>.

SickKids International. "International Patient Office," The Hospital for Sick Children, 1999 2012. Web. 10 July 2012. < http://www.sickkids.ca/sickkidsinternational/38573-SickKids%20IPO%20factsheet%20Nov2011.pdf>.

SickKids International. "International Patient Office," The Hospital for Sick Children, 1999-2012. Web. 10 July 2012. < http://www.sickkids.ca/sickkidsinternational/international-patient-office/index.html>.

SickKids International. "Programme for Global Paediatric Research." The Hospital for Sick Children, 1999-2012. Web. 10 July 2012. <http://www.sickkids.ca/sickkidsinternational/GCHP/PGPR/PGPR.html>.

Appendix A

Fiscal Years Ended March 31	2012	2011	Change
	$	$	%
	(in thousands of dollars)		
STATEMENT OF OPERATIONS			
Revenue	724,808	709,501	2.2%
Expenses	730,525	709,105	3.0%
Excess/(deficiency) of revenue over expenses before investment income	(5,717)	396	
Investment Income	25,194	6,535	285.5%
Excess of revenue over expenses	19,477	6,931	181.0%
BALANCE SHEET			
Assets	1,101,452	939,872	17.2%
Liabilities	1,009,527	867,283	16.4%
Equity	91,925	72,589	26.6%